0 zero

Trace and write the number **0**.

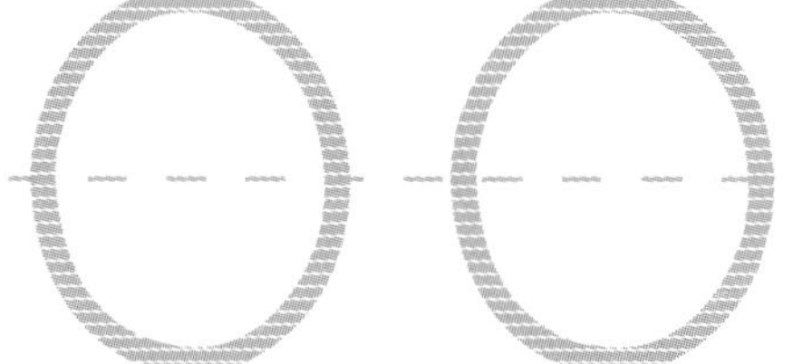

Trace the word **zero**.

zero

Color the dog with **zero** spots.

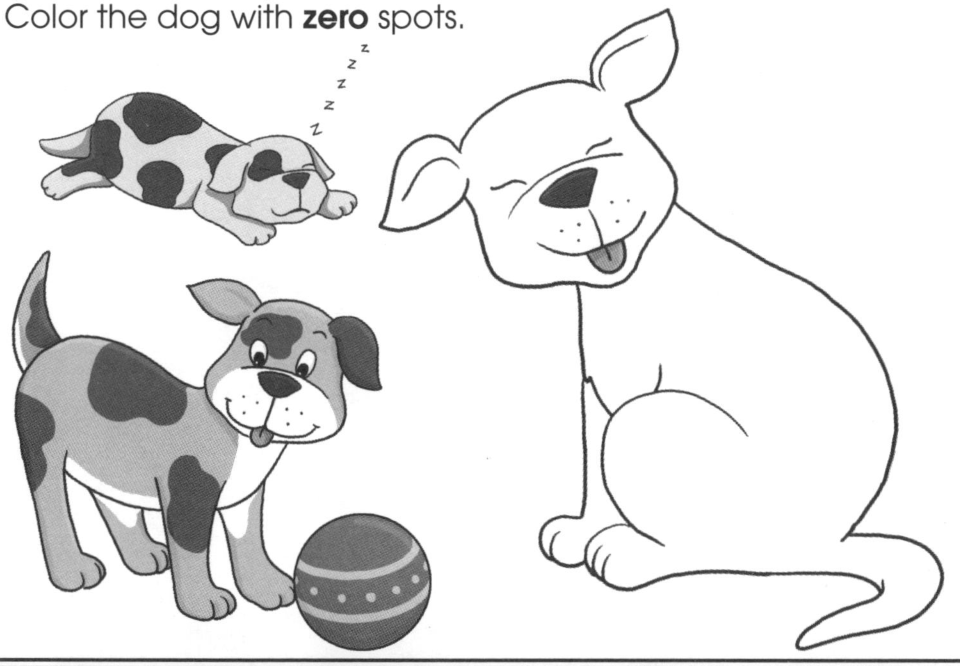

Color the fish with **0** spots orange.

I one

Trace and write I.

Trace the word **one**.

one

Match I with groups of I.

Color **1** picture in each group. Write the number **1** on the line.

2 two

Trace and write **2**.

Trace the word **two**.

Match **2** with groups of **2**.

Make pairs. Draw another to make **2** of each thing.
Color the pictures.

3 three

Trace and write 3.

Trace the word three.

Match 3 with groups of 3.

3

Color **3** candles in each group red.

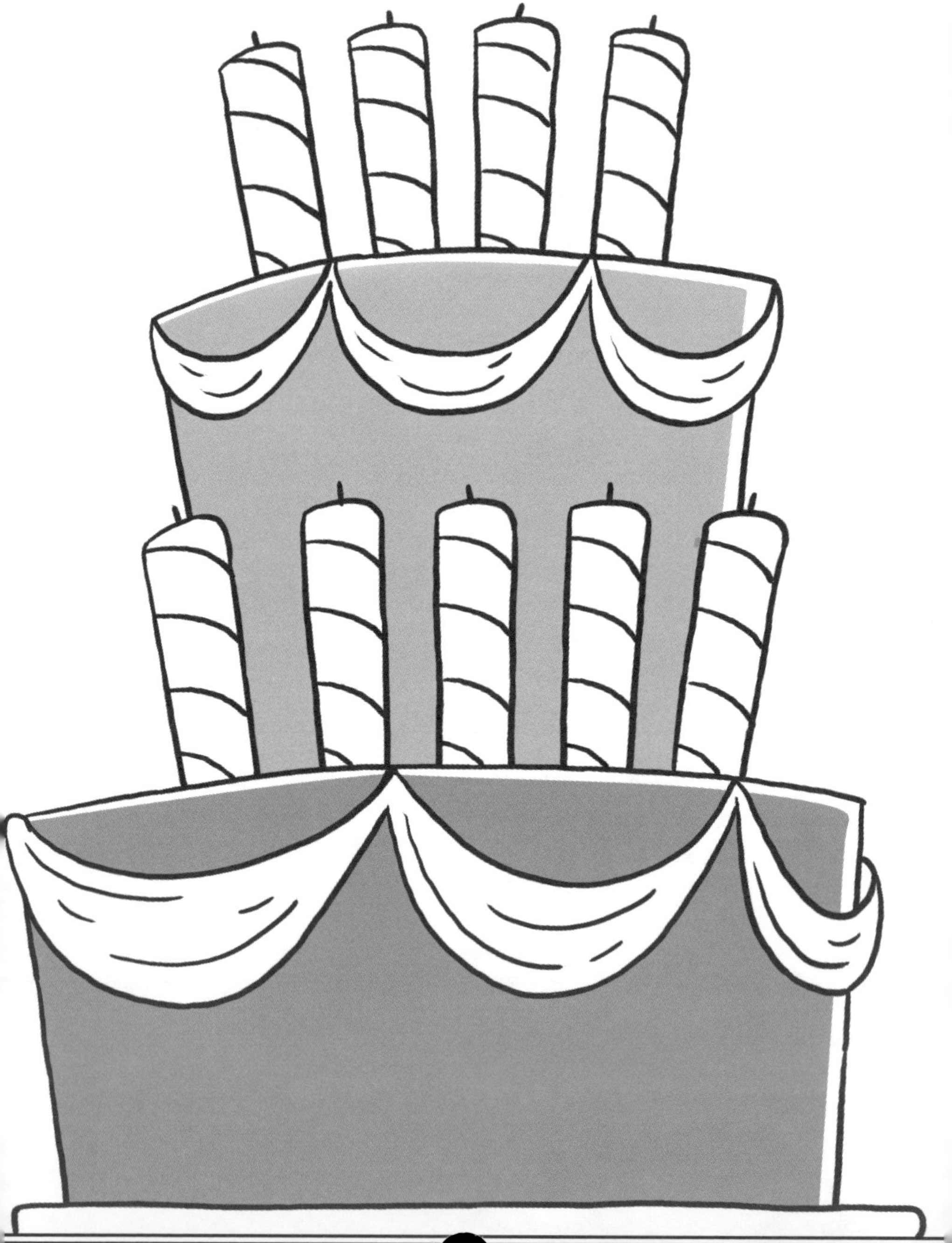

4 four

Trace and write **4**.

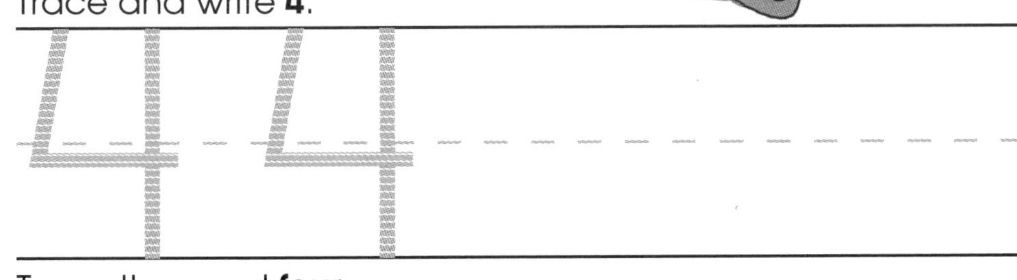

Trace the word **four**.

Match **4** with groups of **4**.

Draw the missing items to show **4** of each kind.
Write the number **4** on each line.

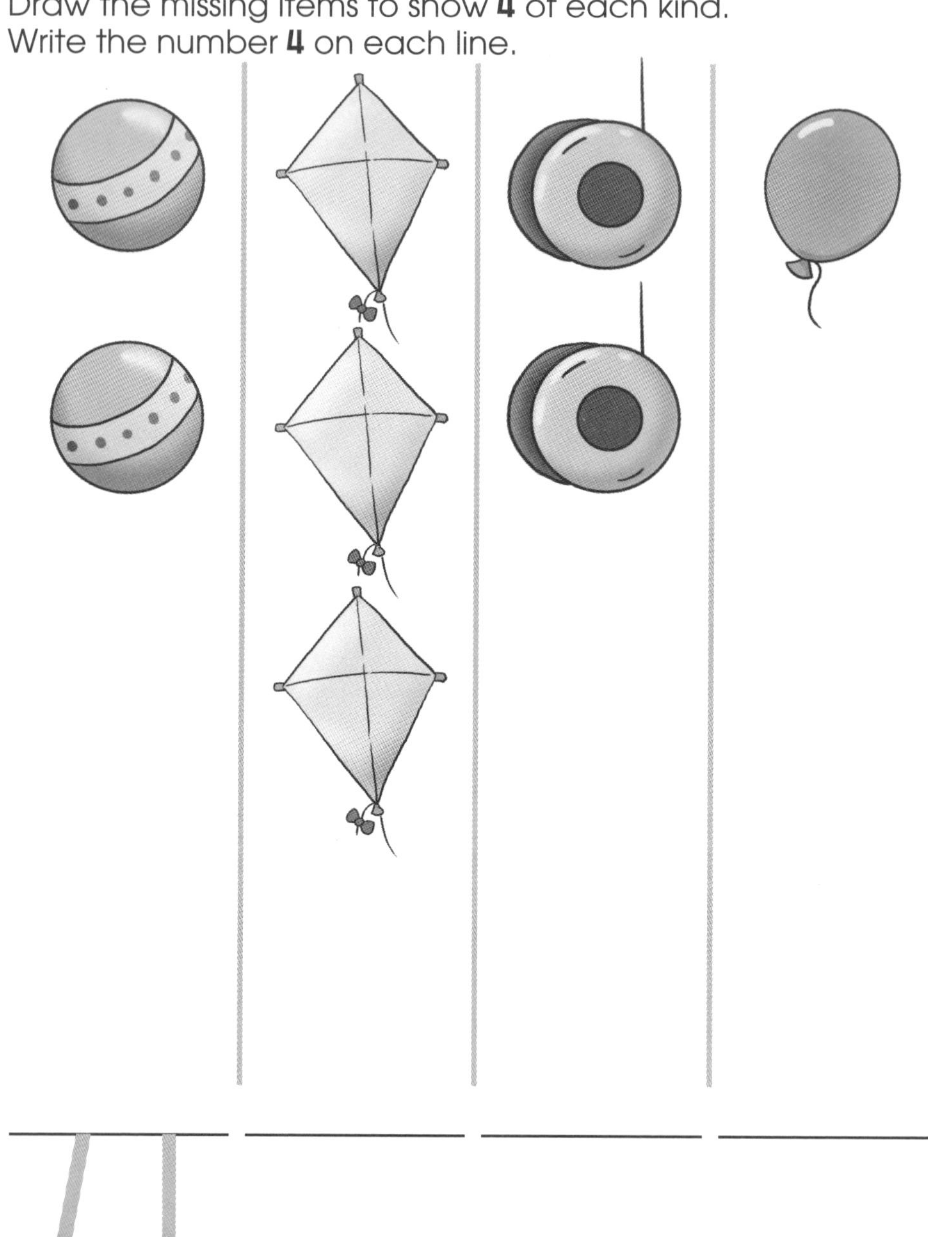

1 2 ③ 4   1 ② 3 4

How many are there? Circle the numbers.

1 2 3 4

1 2 3 4

1 2 3 4

1 2 3 4

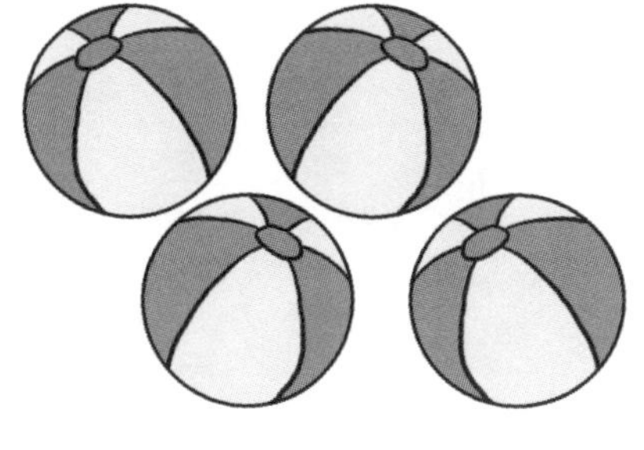

1 2 3 4

1 2 3 4

Draw a line to help each animal find its way home.

How many pigs are now at their home?   1   2   3   4

How many rabbits are now at their home?   1   2   3   4

How many chickens are now at their home?   1   2   3   4

5 five

Trace and write **5**.

Trace the word **five**.

Match **5** with groups of **5**.

Draw the missing items to show **5** of each kind.
Color the pictures.

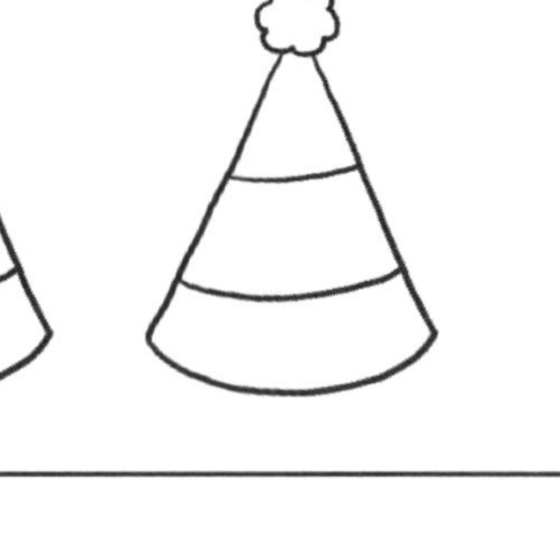

6 six

Trace and write **6**.

6 6

Trace the word **six**.

six

Match **6** with groups of **6**.

6

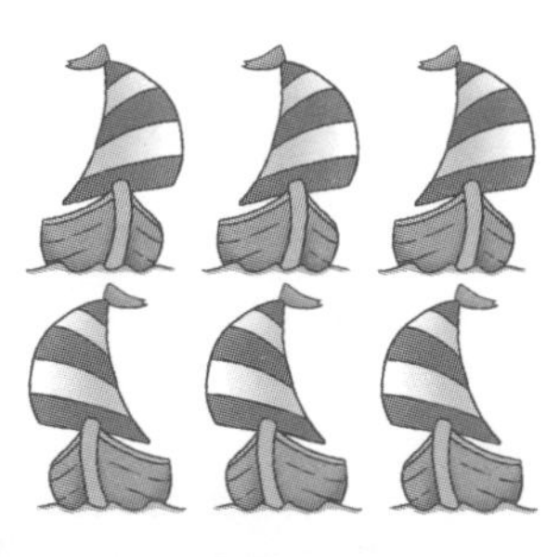

Draw 6  on the tree. Color the apples.

7 **seven**

Trace and write 7.

7 7

Trace the word seven.

seven

Match 7 with groups of 7.

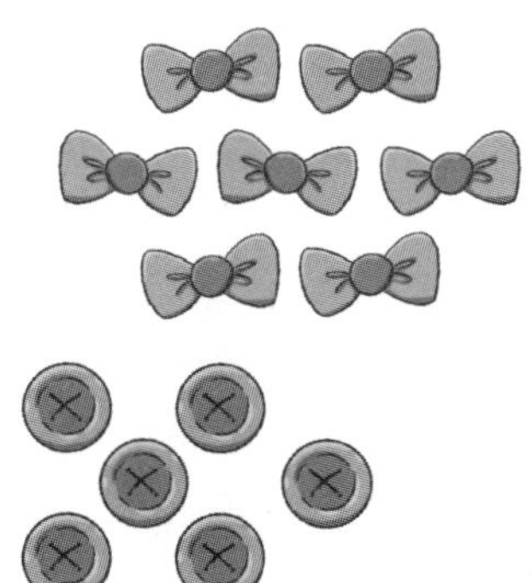

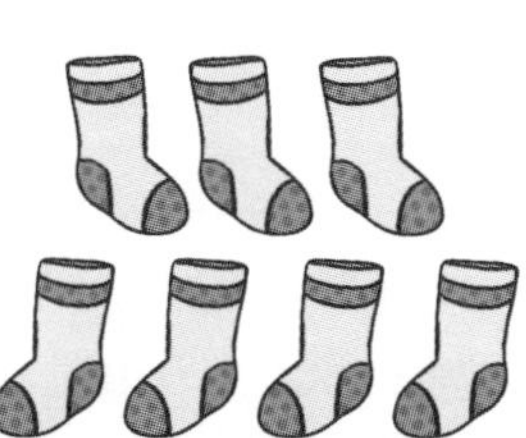

7

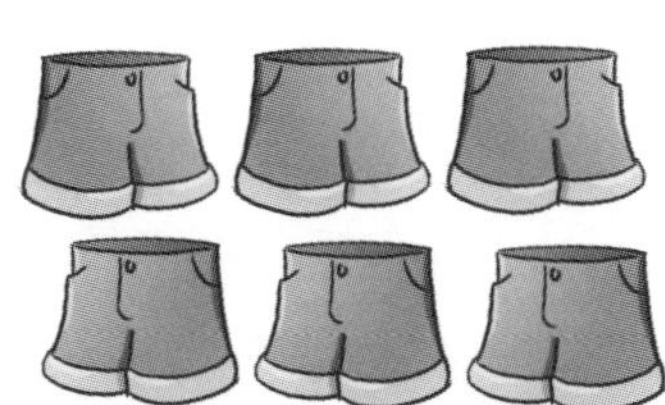

Count the boats.
Draw △ on **7** boats.

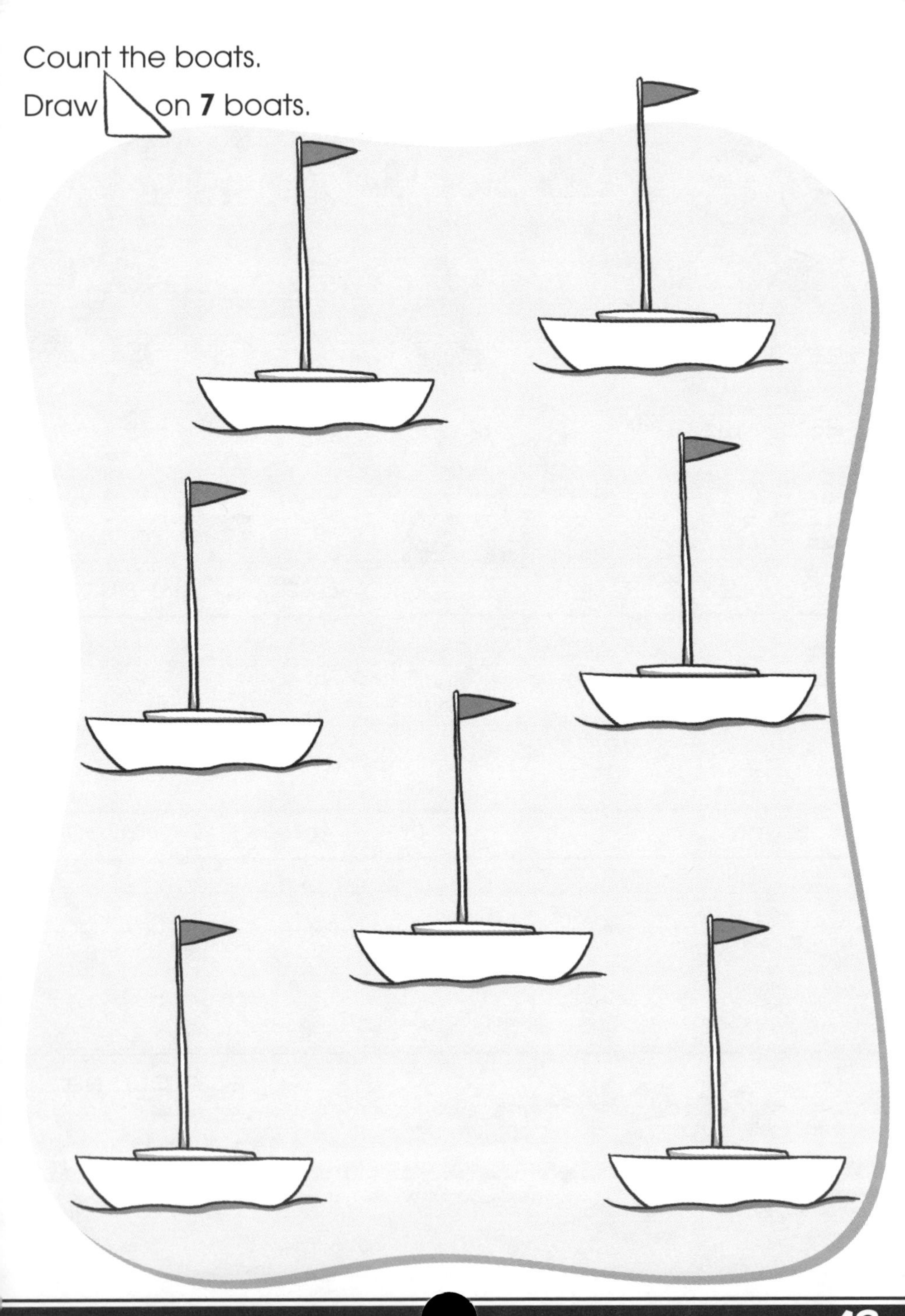

8 eight

Trace and write 8.

Trace the word eight.

Match 8 with groups of 8.

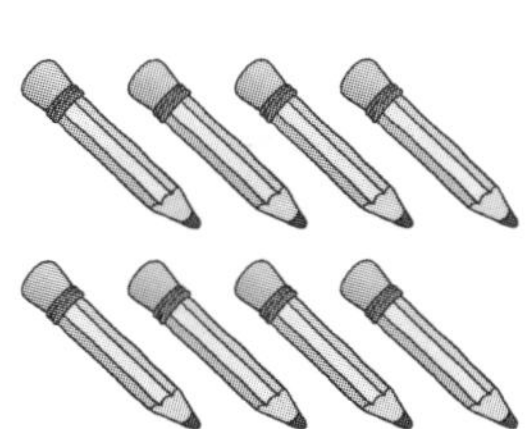

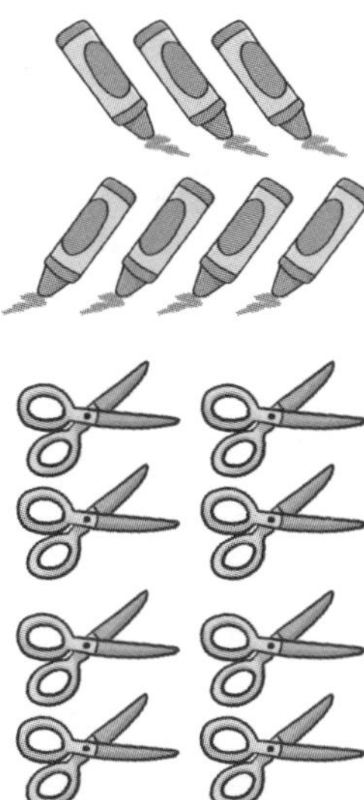

Count each group of insects.
Circle **8** insects in each group.

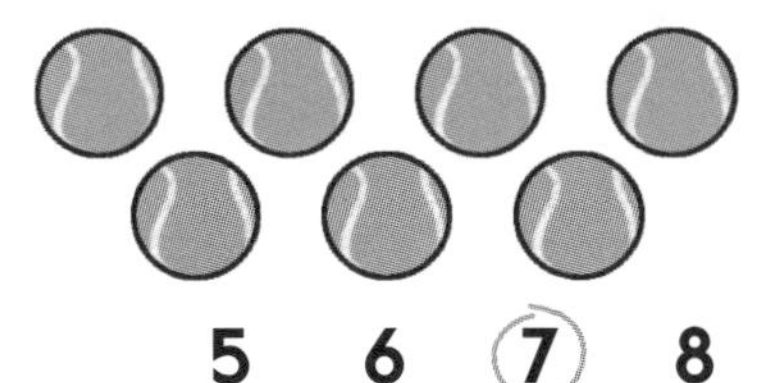

5 6 (7) 8

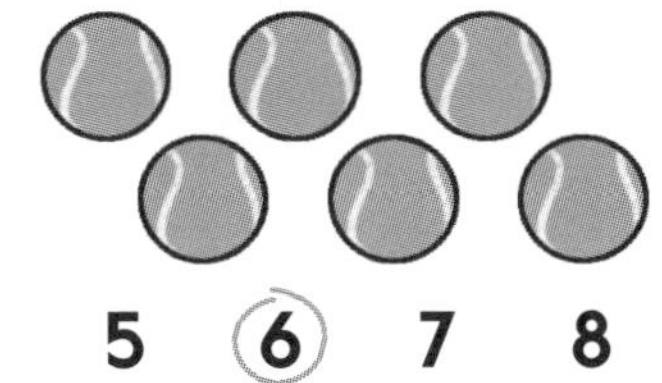

5 (6) 7 8

How many are there? Circle the numbers.

5 6 7 8

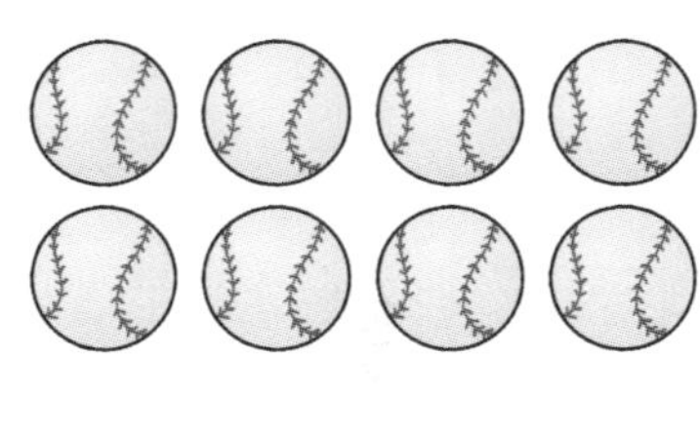

5 6 7 8

5 6 7 8

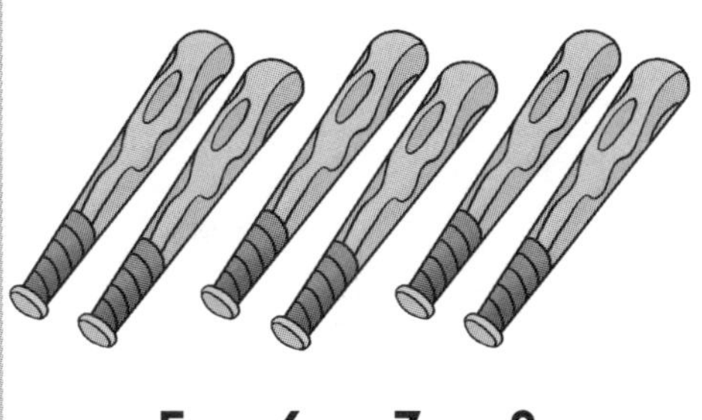

5 6 7 8

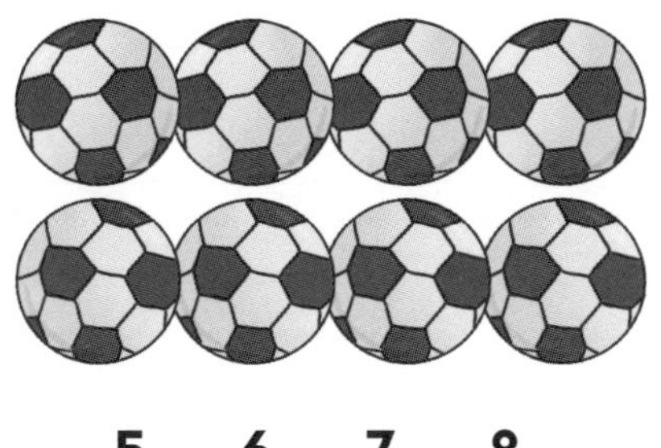

5 6 7 8

5 6 7 8

Color the picture.

5 = green **6 = blue** **7 = purple** **8 = orange**

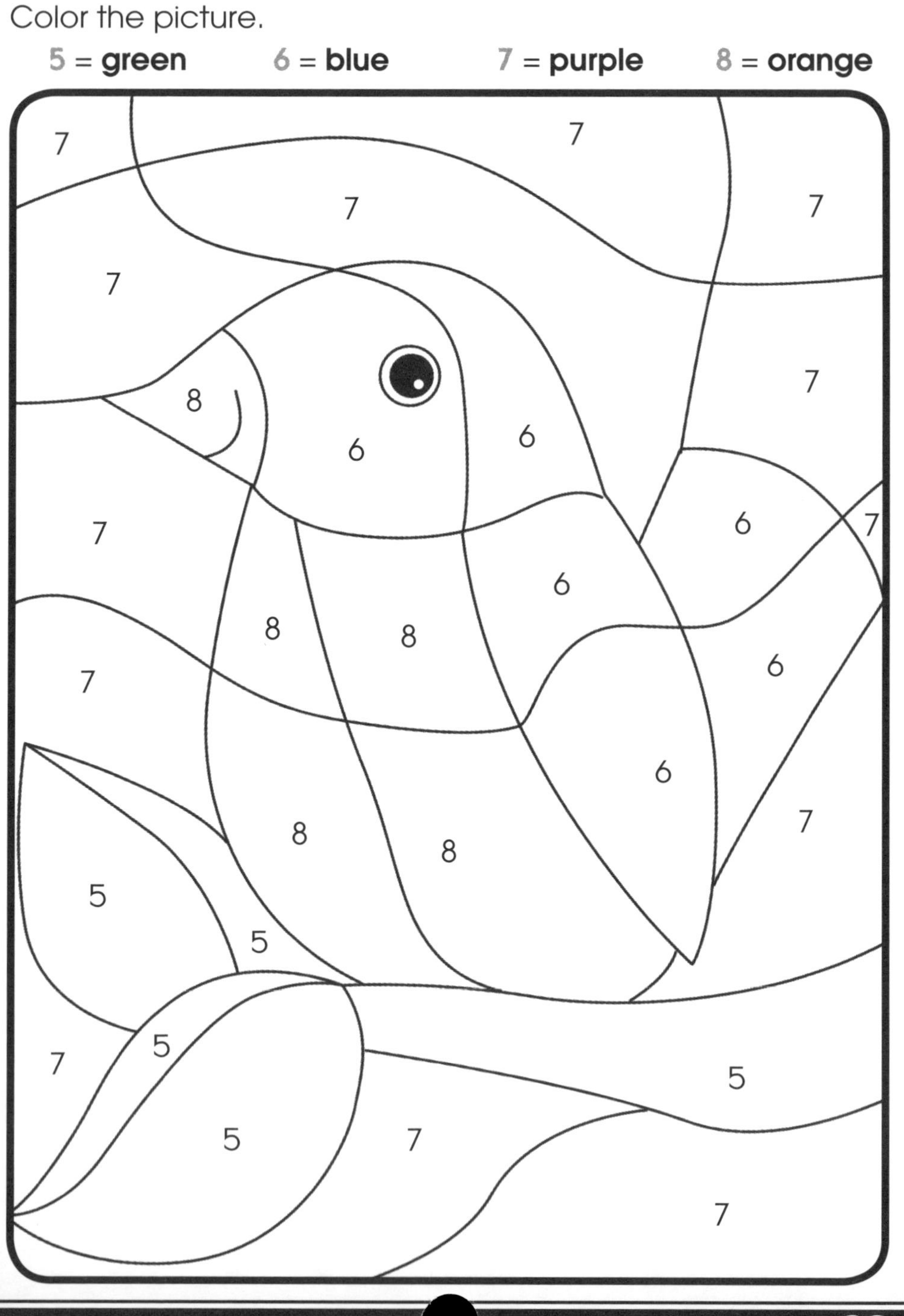

9 nine

Trace and write **9**.

Trace the word **nine**.

Match **9** with groups of **9**.

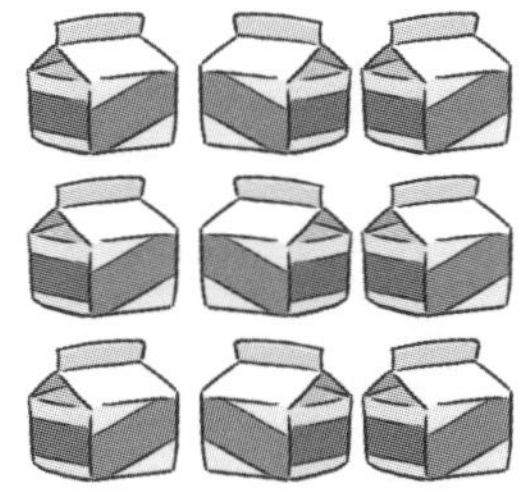
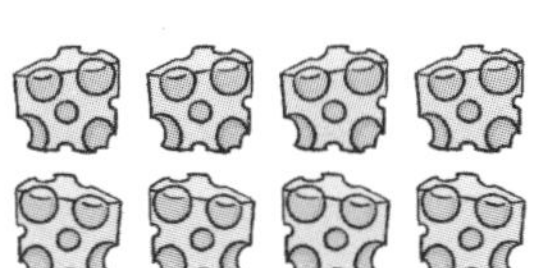

Count each kind of bug.
Circle how many there are.

7 8 9   7 8 9   7 8 9

10 ten

Trace and write **10**.

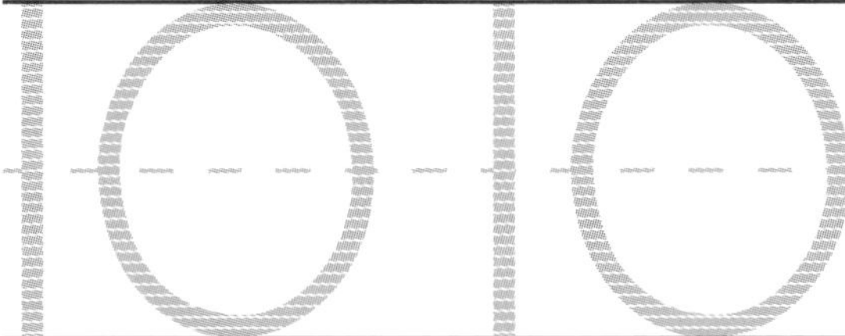

Trace the word **ten**.

Match **10** with groups of **10**.

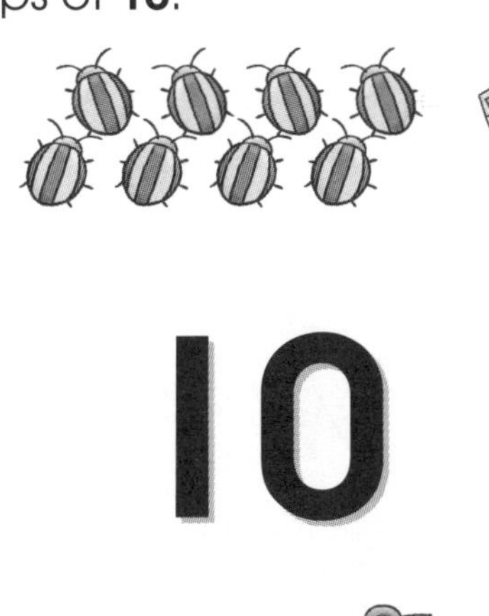

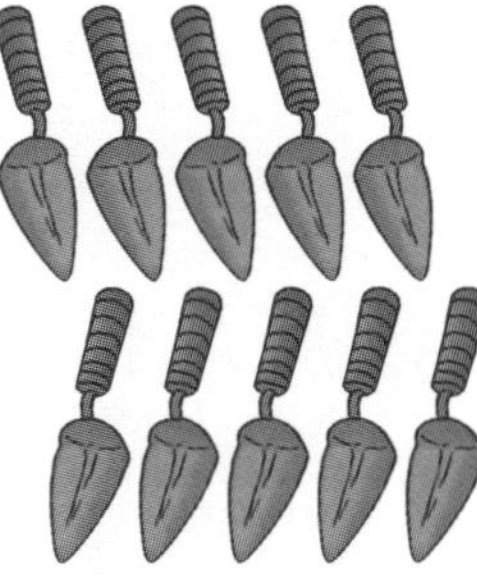

Draw **10** dots on the butterfly. Put **5** dots on each wing.
Color the butterfly.

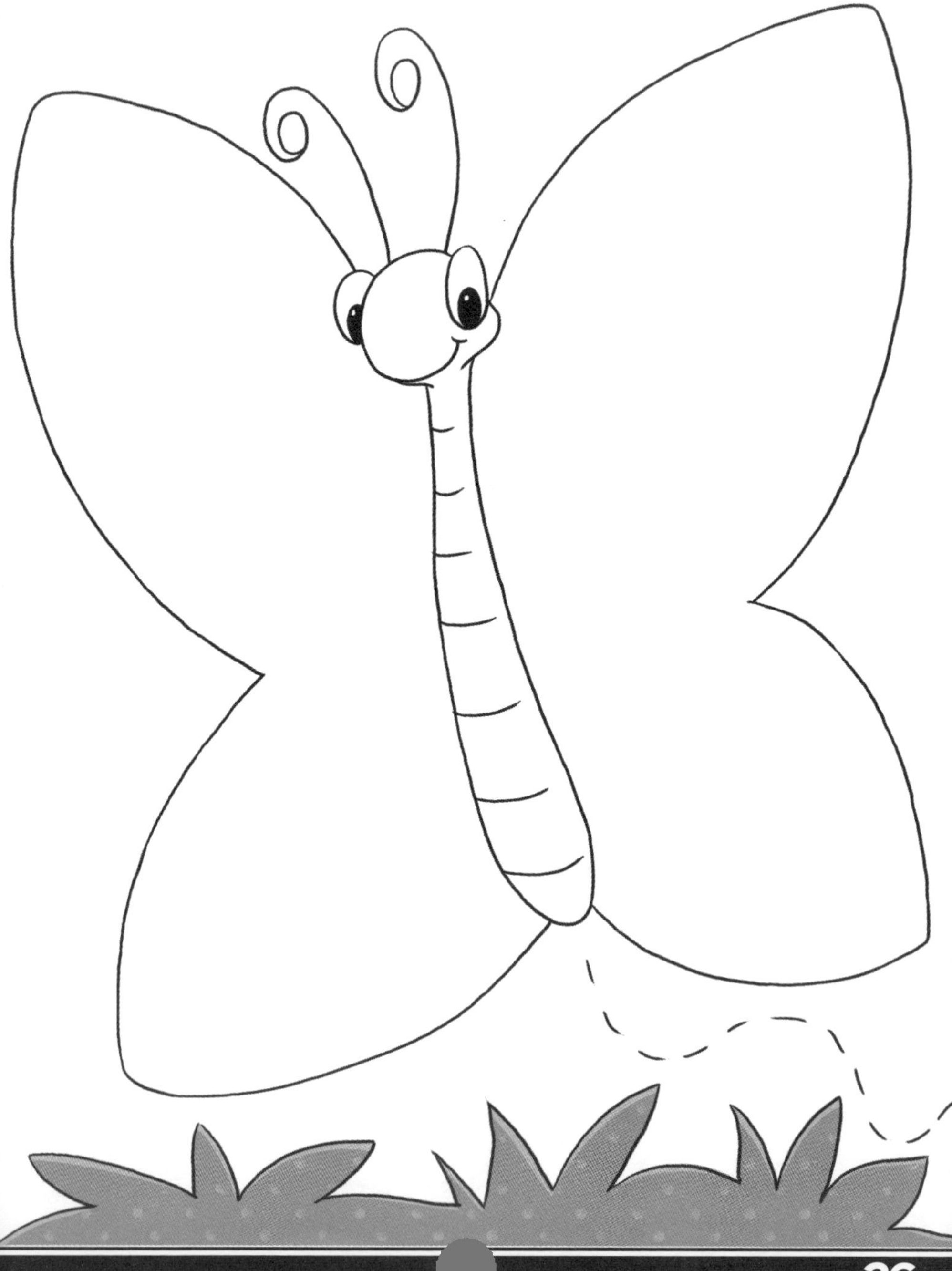

11 eleven

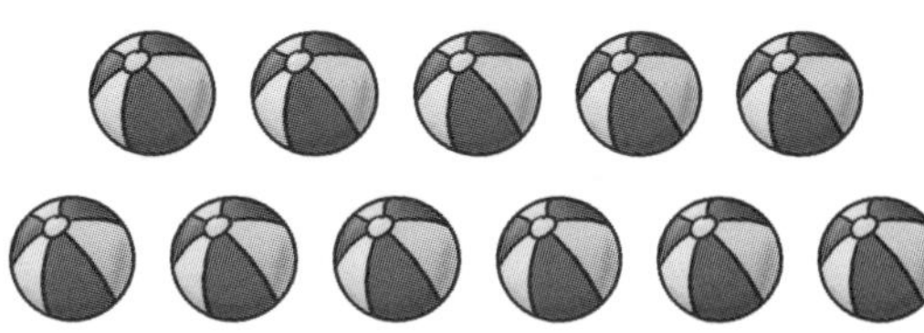

Trace and write 11.

Trace the word **eleven**.

Match 11 with groups of 11.

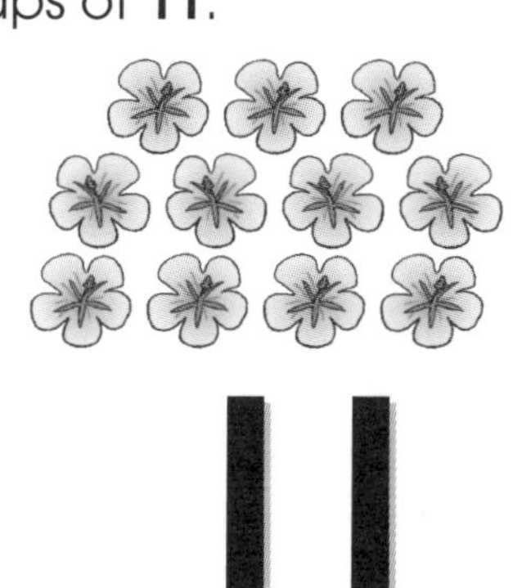

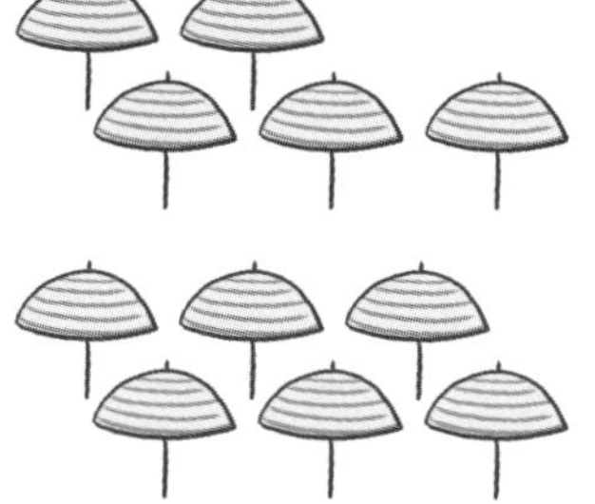

Count the kites.
Color 11 kites.

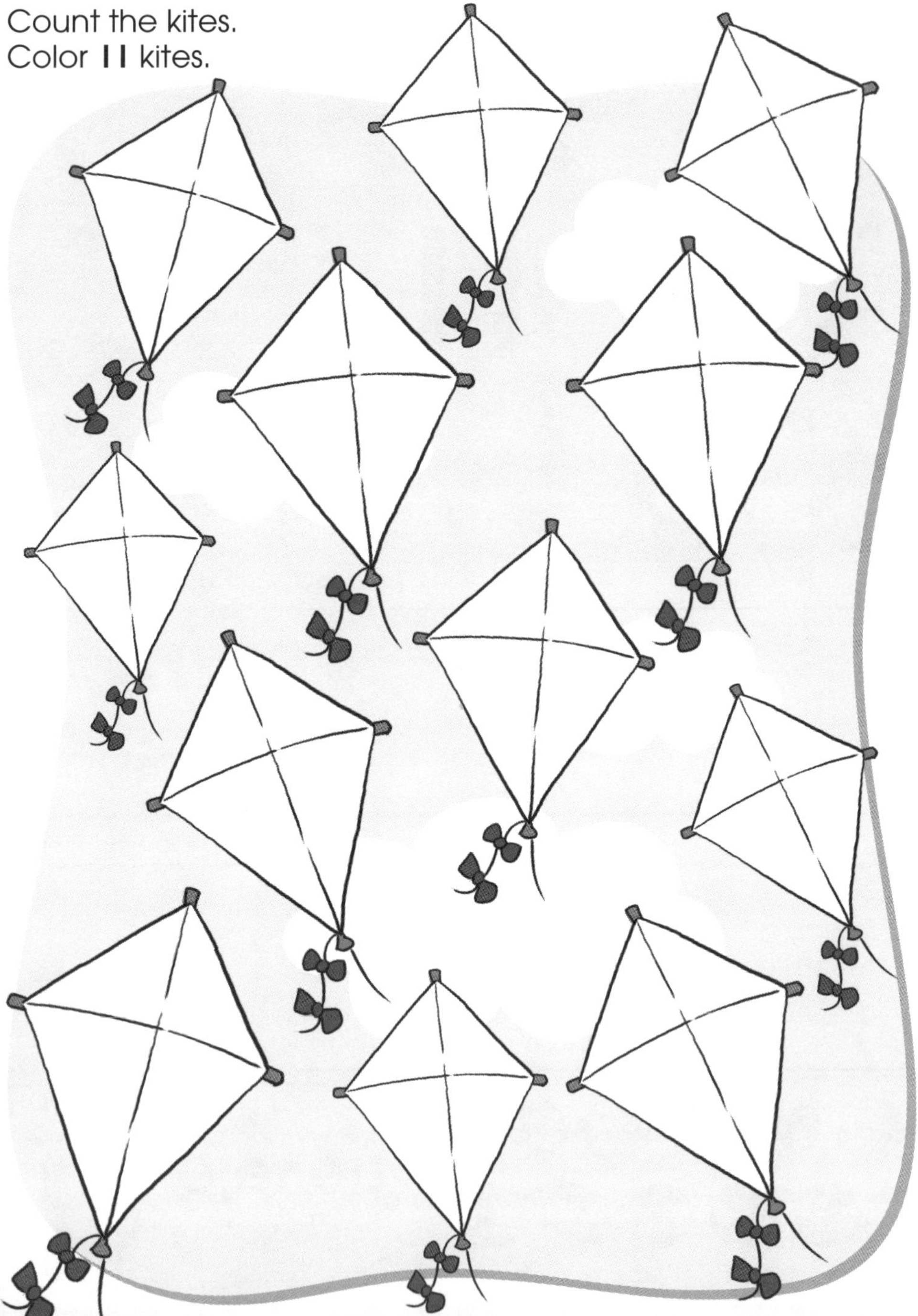

12 twelve

Trace and write **12**.

12 12

Trace the word **twelve**.

twelve

Match **12** with groups of **12**.

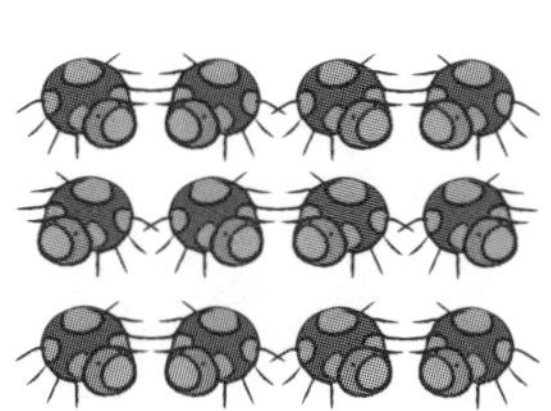

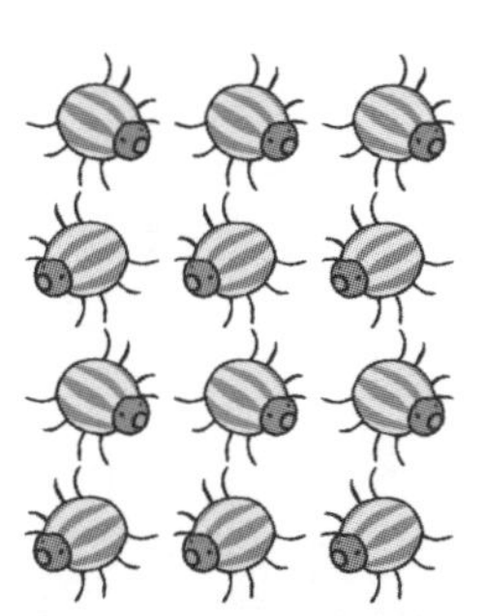

12

Count the strawberries.
Color 12 strawberries.

1 2 3 4 5 6 7 8 9 10 11 12

1

2

3

4

5

6

7

8

9

10

11

12

How many are there? Write the numbers.

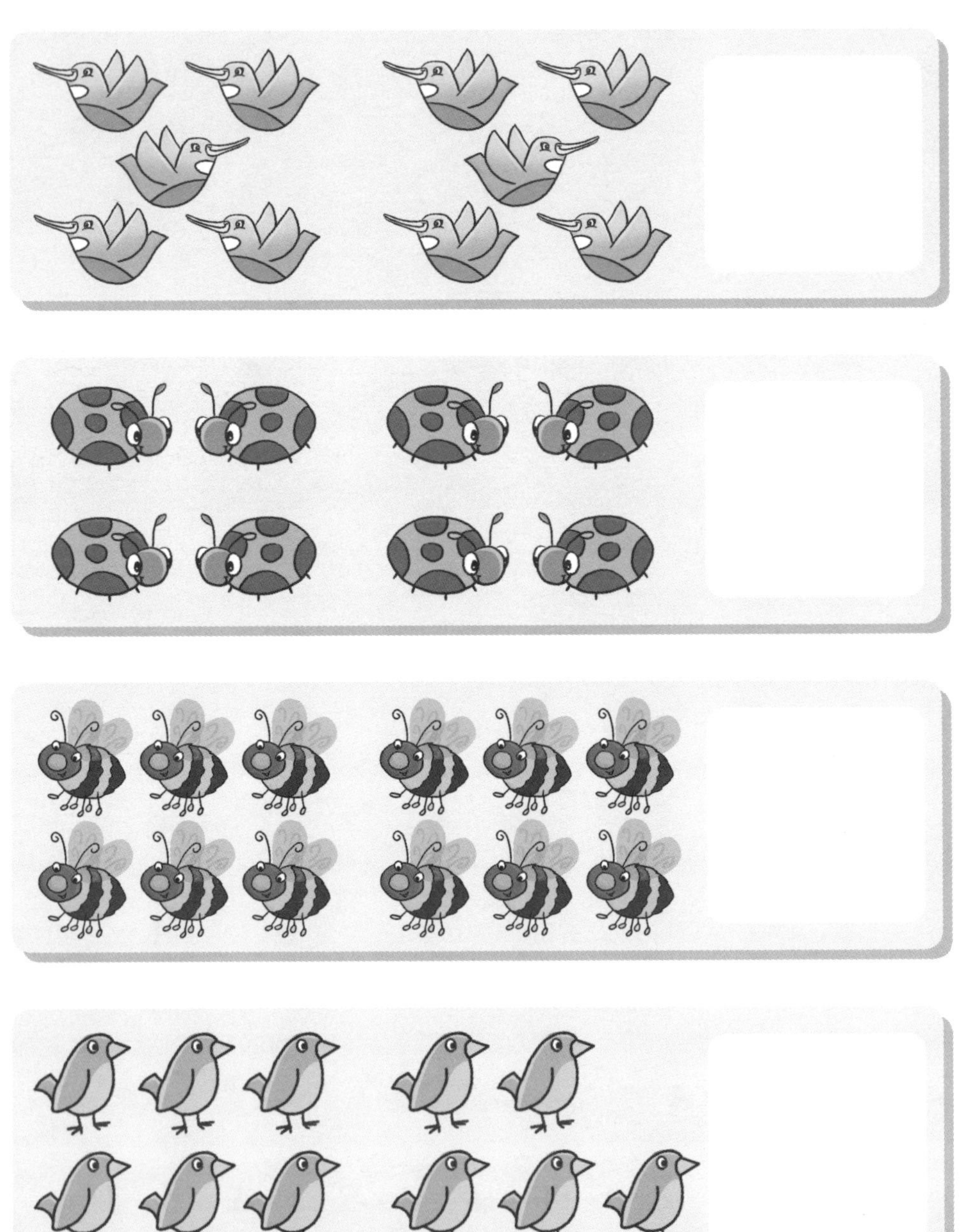

Write the missing numbers from **1** to **12** around
the clock in order.

Write the missing numbers.

1 ___ 3 ___ 5 ___

7 ___ 9 ___ 11 ___

What number comes **next**?

4 5 6 ☐

7 8 9 ☐

0 1 2 ☐

9 10 11 ☐

Write the missing numbers.

3 ☐ ☐ 6

What number comes **before**?

| | 3 | 4 | 5 |

| | 7 | 8 | 9 |

| | 5 | 6 | 7 |

| | 8 | 9 | 10 |

Write the missing numbers.

| | 8 | | | 11 |

Write how many there are.
Circle the set that shows **more**.

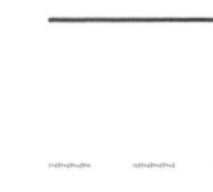

6
3

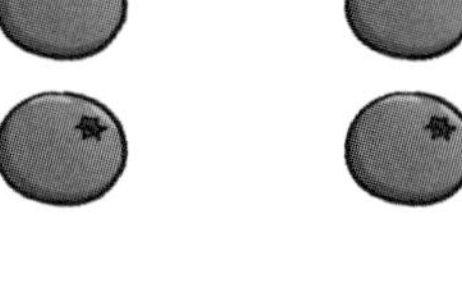
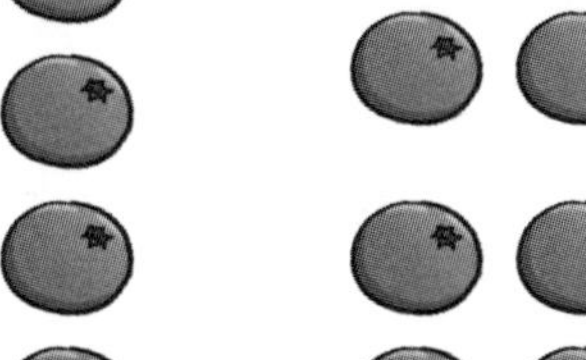

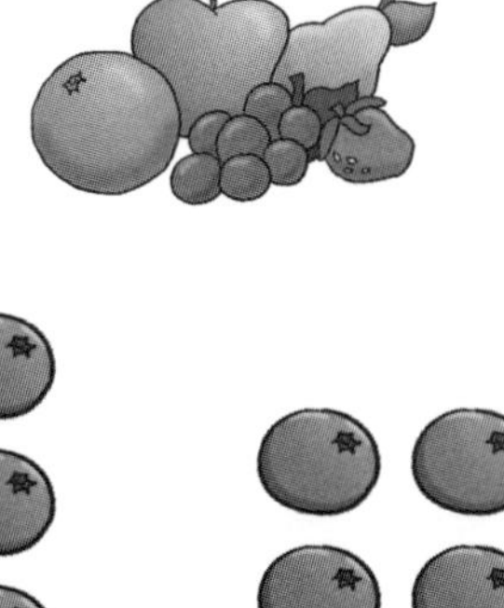

Write how many there are.
Circle the set that shows **fewer**.

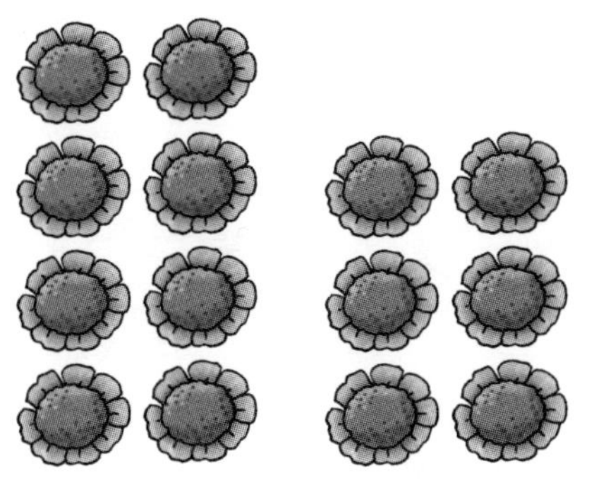

___________________   ___________________

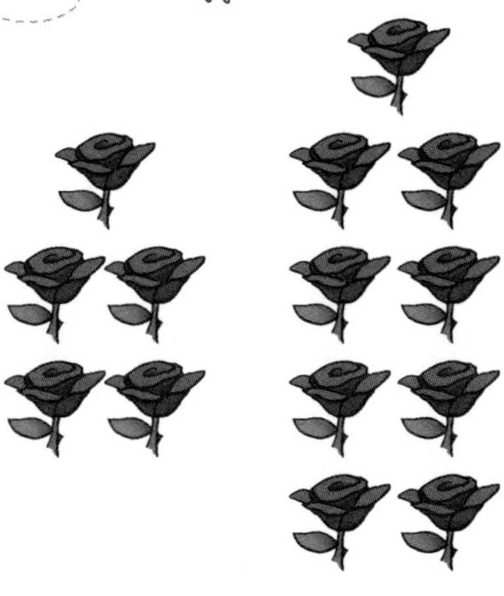

___________________   ___________________

___________________   ___________________

___________________   ___________________

Count the pennies. Write the amounts.

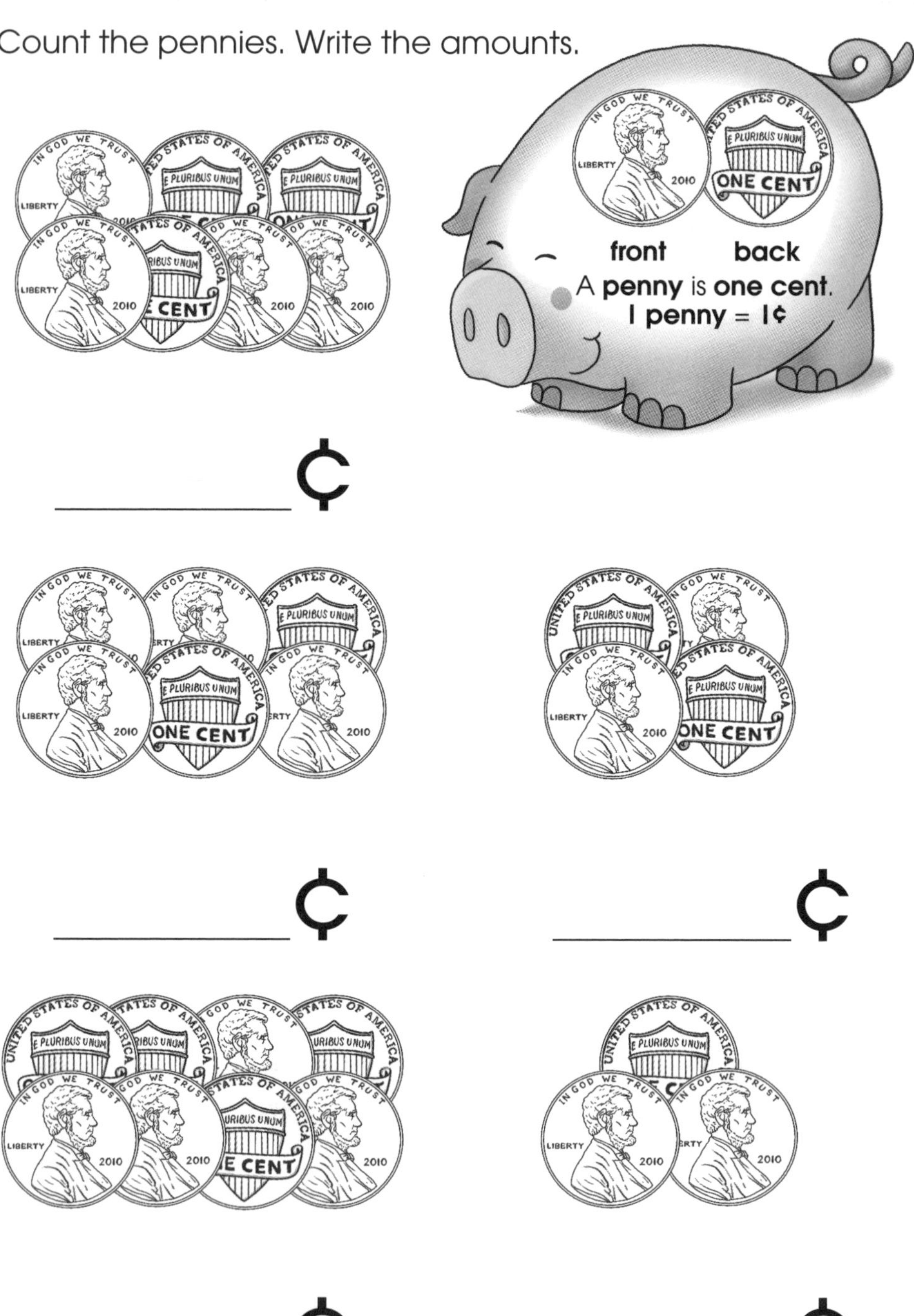

_________ ¢

_________ ¢

_________ ¢

_________ ¢

_________ ¢

How many are there **in all**? Write the numbers.

$2 + 1 = 3$

$1 + 3 = \underline{}$

$3 + 1 = \underline{}$

$2 + 2 = \underline{}$

$2 + 3 = \underline{}$

$3 + 2 = \underline{}$

How many are there **in all**? Write the numbers.

$1 + 1 = \underline{\quad}$

$1 + 4 = \underline{\quad}$

$2 + 2 = \underline{\quad}$

$3 + 1 = \underline{\quad}$

$4 + 1 = \underline{\quad}$

$2 + 0 = \underline{\quad}$

How many are there? Write the number sentences.

2 + 1 = 3

___ + ___ = ___

___ + ___ = ___

How many are there? Write the number sentences.

____ + ____ = ____

____ + ____ = ____

____ + ____ = ____

How many are **left**? Write the numbers.

$3 - 1 = \underline{2}$ 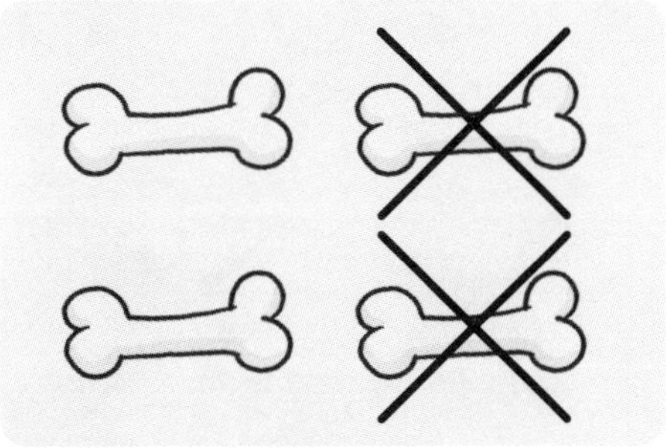 $4 - 2 = \underline{}$

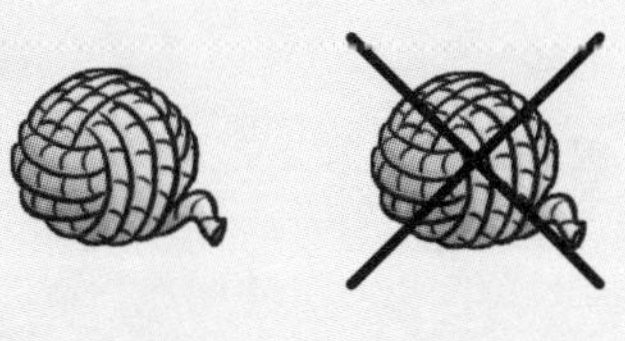

$5 - 2 = \underline{}$ $2 - 1 = \underline{}$

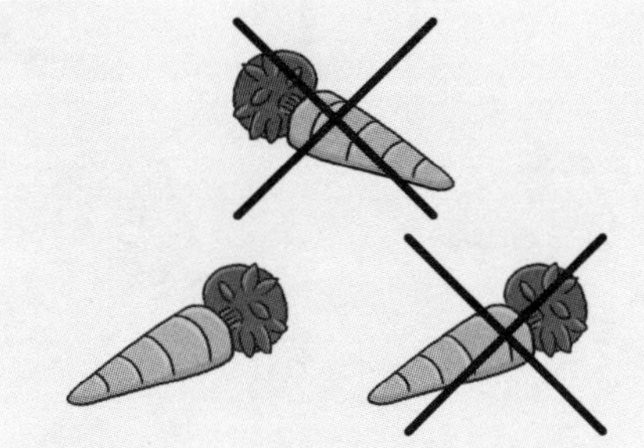

$4 - 1 = \underline{}$ $3 - 2 = \underline{}$

How many are **left**? Write the numbers.

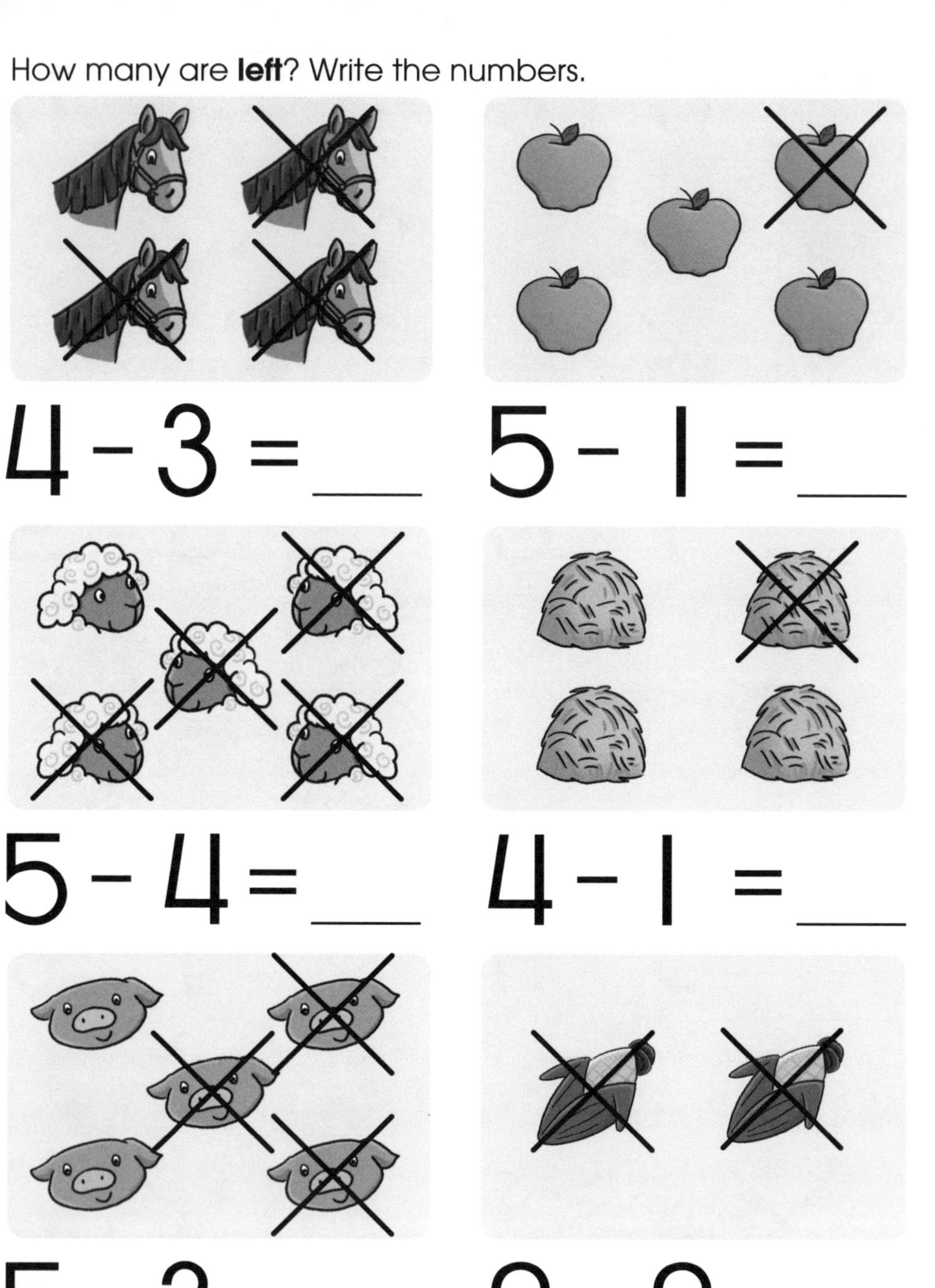

$4 - 3 =$ ___ $5 - 1 =$ ___

$5 - 4 =$ ___ $4 - 1 =$ ___

$5 - 3 =$ ___ $2 - 2 =$ ___

How many are there? Write the numbers.

3 in all   1 going away   2 are left

_______   _______   _______

in all   going away   is left

_______   _______   _______

in all   going away   are left

_______   _______   _______

How many are there? Write the number sentences.

$$2 - 1 = 1$$

$$\underline{} - \underline{} = \underline{}$$

$$\underline{} - \underline{} = \underline{}$$

Trace each shape.
Color each shape.
Draw lines to match the shapes.

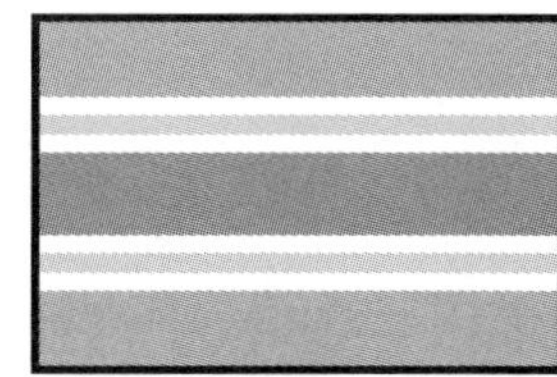

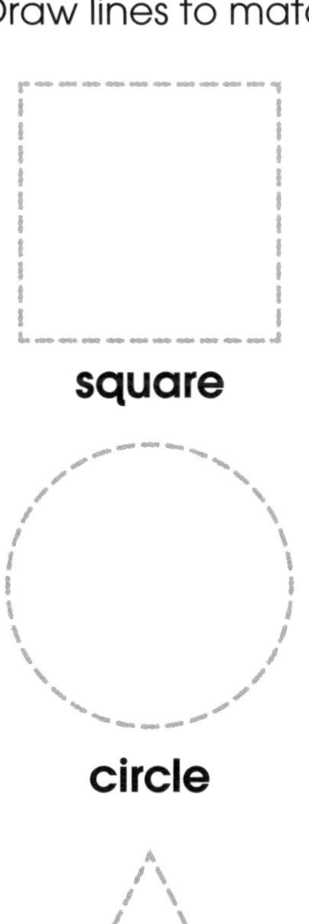

square

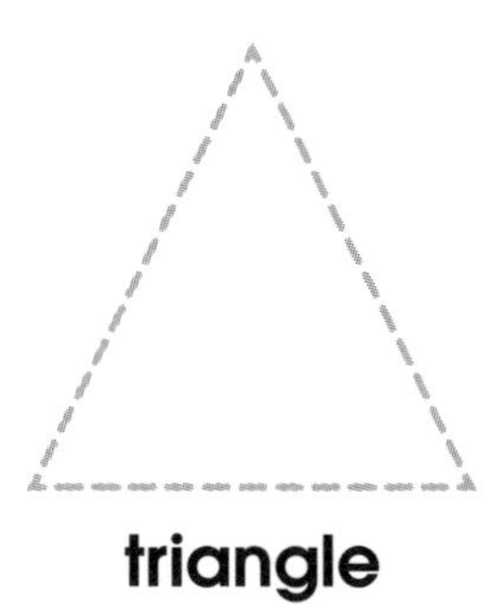

circle

triangle

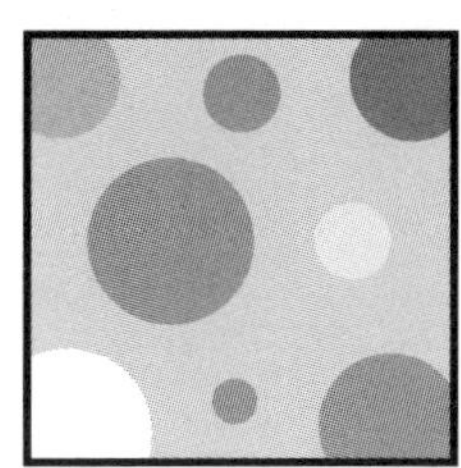

rectangle

Draw what comes **next** in each pattern. Color your patterns.

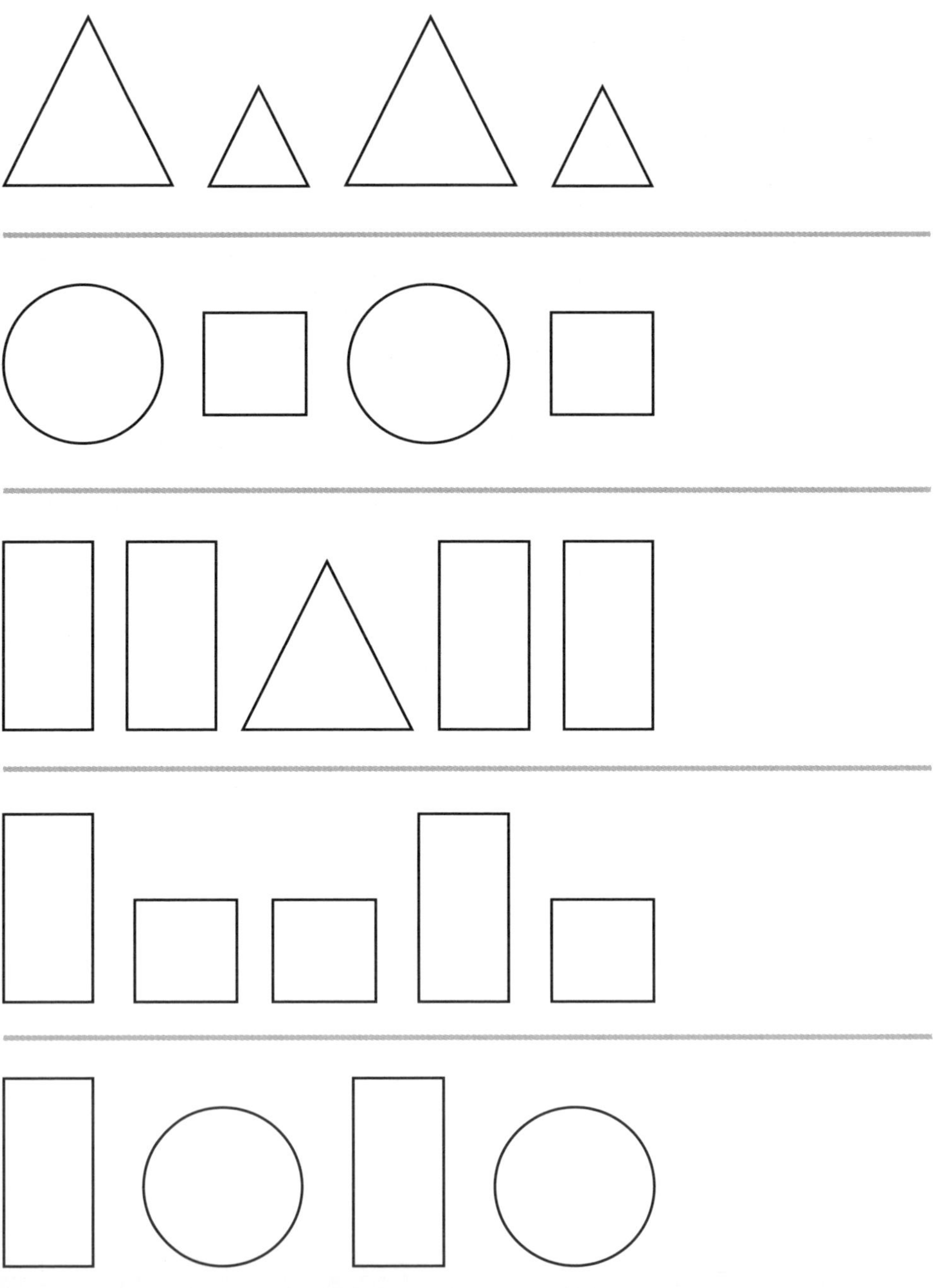